Jupiter

by J.P. Bloom

ABDO
PLANETS
Kids

abdopublishing.com

Published by Abdo Kids, a division of ABDO, PO Box 398166, Minneapolis, Minnesota 55439.

Printed in the United States of America, North Mankato, Minnesota.

102014

012015

 THIS BOOK CONTAINS
RECYCLED MATERIALS

Photo Credits: iStock, NASA, Science Source, Shutterstock, Thinkstock

Production Contributors: Teddy Borth, Jennie Forsberg, Grace Hansen

Design Contributors: Candice Keimig, Laura Rask, Dorothy Toth

Library of Congress Control Number: 2014943796

Cataloging-in-Publication Data

J.P. Bloom.

 Jupiter / J.P. Bloom.

  p. cm. -- (Planets)

ISBN 978-1-62970-716-7 (lib. bdg.)

Includes index.

1. Jupiter (Planet)--Juvenile literature. 2. Solar system--Juvenile literature. I. Title.

523.45--dc23

2014943796

Table of Contents

Jupiter

Jupiter is a **planet**. Planets **orbit** stars. Planets in our solar system orbit the sun.

Jupiter is the fifth closest **planet** to the sun. It is about 484 million miles (779 million km) away from the sun.

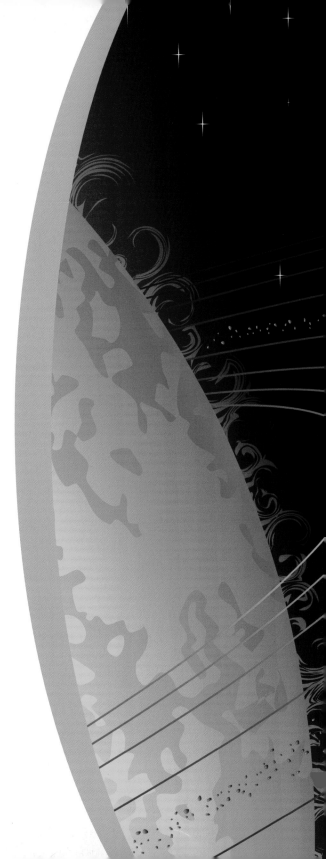

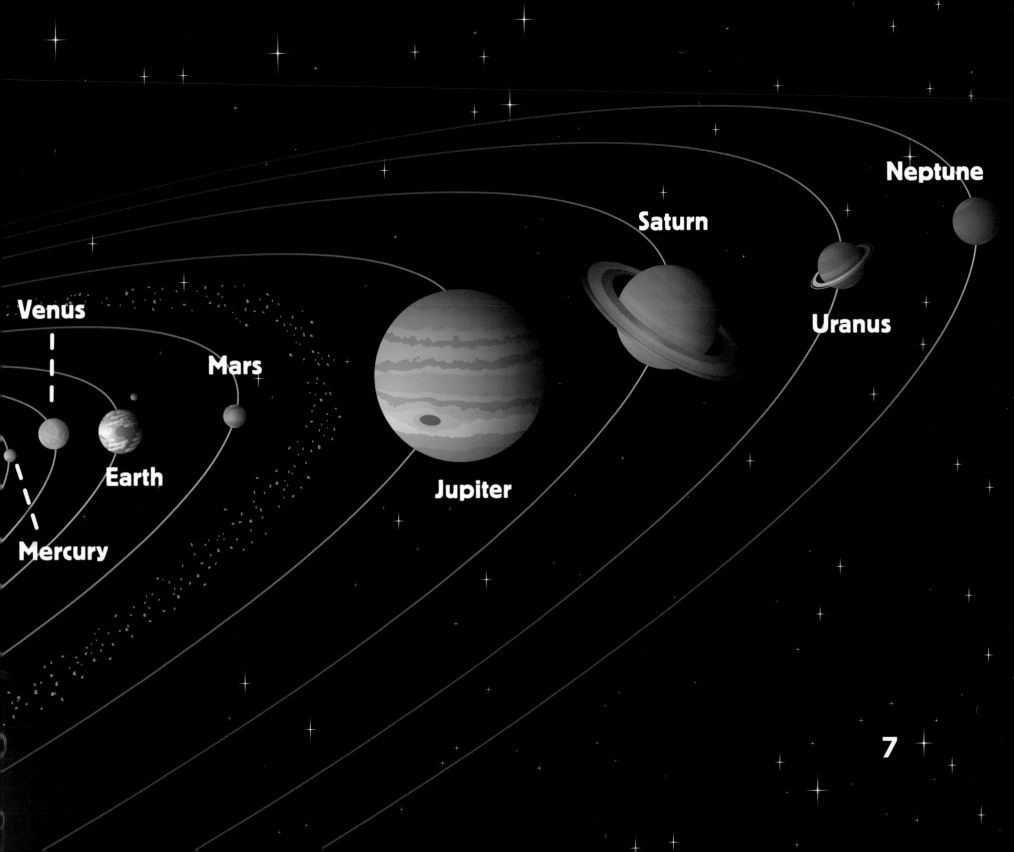

Venus

Mars

Neptune

Saturn

Uranus

Earth

Jupiter

Mercury

7

Jupiter **orbits** the sun very slowly. One year on Jupiter is about 12 years on Earth.

Io
(moon)

Europa
(moon)

Jupiter spins while it **orbits** the sun. The spin makes day and night. Jupiter spins very fast. One day on Jupiter is about 10 hours on Earth.

**Europa
(moon)**

Jupiter is the largest planet in our solar system. It is 2.5 times bigger than all of the planets combined!

Earth
7,918 miles
(12,742 km)

Jupiter   86,881 miles   (139,822 km)

Jupiter is a giant ball of gas.

You cannot stand on Jupiter.

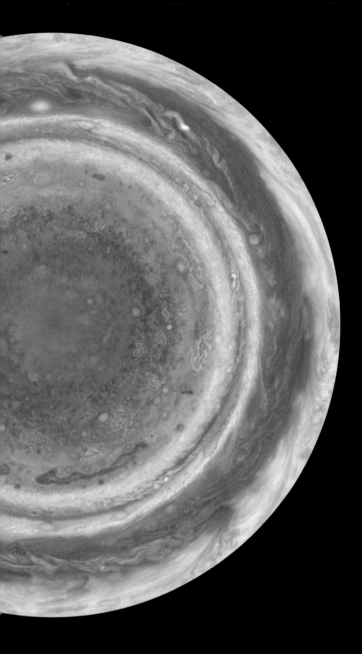

South Pole

North Pole

15

Stormy Planet

Jupiter has many storms.

There is lightning on Jupiter.

There are very fast winds too.

17

There is a red spot on Jupiter.

This spot is one giant storm.

It has lasted for hundreds

of years!

WFC3 / UVIS
April 21, 2014

1995 WFPC2

2009 WFC3 / UVIS

2014 WFC3 / UVIS

Jupiter from Earth

You can see Jupiter in the night's sky.

Venus

Jupiter

21

More Facts

- Jupiter has rings. It is believed by scientists that the rings are made from Jupiter's moons.

- Jupiter has many moons. There were 67 known moons as of 2014. Its moon Ganymede is bigger around than Mercury!

- Jupiter is very large. Its **gravity** pulls space objects toward it. Jupiter is sometimes called "the solar system's vacuum cleaner."

Glossary

combined – put together.

gravity – a natural force that pulls objects downward.

orbit – the path of a space object as it moves around another space object. To orbit is to follow this path.

planet – a large, round object in space (such as Earth) that travels around a star (such as the sun).

Index

abdokids.com

Use this code to log on to abdokids.com and access crafts, games, videos, and more!

Abdo Kids Code:
PJK7167